This Book Is
Presented to

_____

_____

_____

_____

_____

The Virtuous Woman

YOUR GUIDE TO TRUE FEMINISM

DAVID L. JOHNSTON

COPYRIGHT

HigherLife Development Services, Inc.
P.O. Box 623307
Oviedo, Florida 32762
(407) 563-4806
www.ahigherlife.com

Cover design by Bill Johnson
Interior by Faithe Thomas
Images from DepositPhotos.com

The Virtuous Woman
ISBN 978-1-958211-01-4 (hardback)

Printed in the United States of America
10 9 8 7 6 5 4 3 2 1

A Gracious Woman Retains Honor

Proverbs 31: 10–31

Who can find a virtuous woman (KJV)? For her worth is far above rubies.

The heart of her husband safely trusts her; so he will have no lack of gain.

She does him good and not evil all the days of her life.

She seeks wool and flax, and willingly works with her hands.

She is like the merchant ships, she brings her food from afar.

She also rises while it is yet night, and provides food for her household, and a portion for her maidservants.

She considers a field and buys it; from her profits she plants a vineyard.

She girdeth her loins with strength (KJV), and strengthens her arms.

She perceives that her merchandise is good, and her lamp does not go out by night.

She stretches out her hands to the distaff, and her hand holds the spindle.

She extends her hand to the poor, yes, she reaches out her hands to the needy.

She is not afraid of snow for her household, for all her household is clothed with scarlet.

She makes tapestry for herself; her clothing is fine linen and purple.

Her husband is known in the gates, when he sits among the elders of the land.

She makes linen garments and sells them, and supplies sashes for the merchants.

Strength and honor are her clothing; she shall rejoice in time to come.

She opens her mouth with wisdom, and on her tongue is the law of kindness.

She watches over the ways of her household, and does not eat the bread of idleness.

Her children rise up and call her blessed; her husband also, and he praises her: "Many daughters have done well, but you excel them all."

Charm is deceitful and beauty is passing, but a woman who fears the Lord, she shall be praised.

Give her of the fruit of her hands, and let her own works praise her in the gates.

And God said, "It is not good that man should be alone."

GENESIS
— 2:18 —

THE VALUE OF WOMEN

It is said that when God brought Eve to Adam and Adam saw her for the first time, he said, "WOW-MAN!" Thus the term, "Woman." Since then, however, it seems that women have been viewed unjustly.

Some of these judgments (primarily those from a male perspective) have been prejudiced and harmful. As a result, women have been undervalued, underestimated, underappreciated, underpaid, under-everything. The paradox is that women have been treated as beasts of burden—even while they served and raised their households!

For centuries, men have treated women like chattel. A multitude have been used to satisfy men's lust only to be discarded like tattered coats—with no thought to their well-being. Men have moved from one woman to another, and then another, and yet another, using and abusing as they go.

Some cultures have tried to dignify this practice by requiring a man to marry each one, establishing polygamy. One woman is never esteemed sufficient to complete one man. He needs more. Today this continues in another form: Men still want intimate relationships with women, but they do not want to commit, so they go from woman to woman regularly without marrying. Crushed by this reality, in a culture set on legalizing immorality, coupled with an entertainment business that shamelessly portrays disgusting relationships, women have been forced to fight back. Unfortunately, some have reduced themselves to the same shameless behaviors they have seen. What a tragedy!

An anonymous writer said, "When the men of a society become immoral, that's one thing. But when the women of that society become immoral, there is no return."

Still, women have been the moral fiber holding culture together since time began. Women have been the favorite subject of the poet's pen, while artists have mixed paint and pigment, brush and canvas to capture their smile and likeness. Adored as mothers, they have no rival in some areas. Stemming from their caring nature, women have excelled in many ways. They began nursing and still dominate that vocation. Some even view women as the new and improved version of a man. As someone humorously remarked, "God created man before woman—but there is always a rough draft before the masterpiece." Women are the heart of every family in the world.

Even so, recently men have been trying to pull women down off even this pedestal and into their gutter. Today women are judged by a perverted sense of values (or should I say, lack of values). The lengths men have gone to get women to bow to their monstrous egos and undisciplined libidos is disgusting. Their deceit and manipulation has been dreadful, and women have paid dearly.

"MEN,
Take care not to
make women weep,
for God counts
their tears."

THOMAS S. MONSON

"WOMEN are the real architects of society."

HARRIET BEECHER STOWE

However, chivalry is not altogether dead. There have always been some real men. They are not just from the "days of old when men were bold." There are still men that maintain high standards of character and conduct. Real men are valiant, courageous, strong, and humble, so they are courteous, loyal, generous, and unselfish—especially towards women.

They are not for sale and cannot be bought by money or a cheap sensual thrill. They are sound from center to circumference, and need to be leading the way in treating women properly today.

So what is the ideal woman? How do we find the balance in the midst of the polarized viewpoints of our time? The world does not offer anything definitive for us to follow.

That's the question before us. Is there a definition? If so, where can it be found?

For starters, a virtuous woman is free from vice, immorality, and wickedness, but there is much more. As I've searched, I failed to find any definitions comparable to those found in the book of Proverbs. A proverb is a wise maxim, often of ancient origin, that teaches us truths on a deep level. There are twenty-eight characteristics outlined in Proverbs 31 that describe a virtuous woman. I'm sure you will agree that this kind of woman is the ultimate in true feminism! Let's look at Proverbs 31!

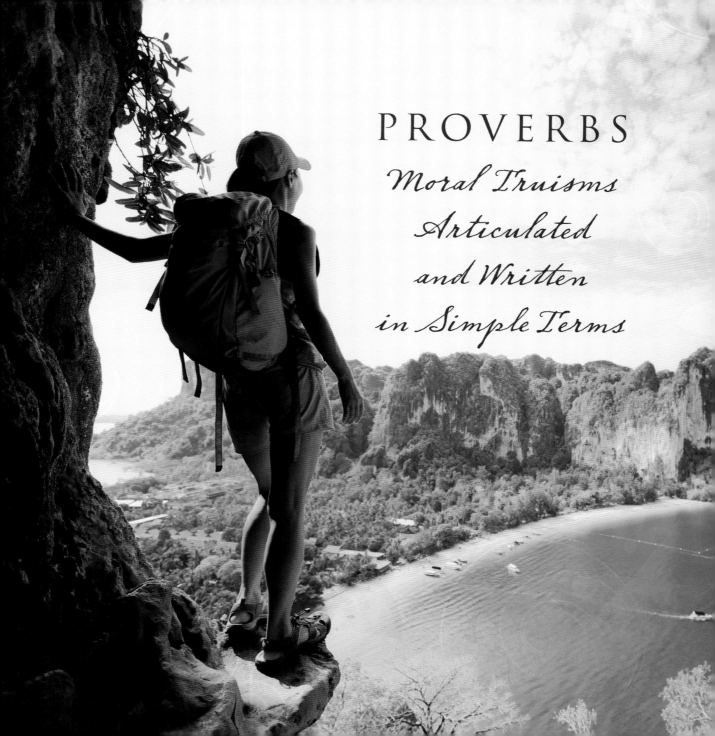

PROVERBS

*Moral Truisms
Articulated
and Written
in Simple Terms*

THE PURPOSE OF PROVERBS

Proverbs 31

Proverbs are: "Written down so we'll know how to live well and right, to understand what life means and where it's going; a manual for living, for learning what's right and just and fair; to teach the inexperienced the ropes and give our young people a grasp on reality.

"There's something here also for seasoned men and women, still a thing or two for the experienced to learn; fresh wisdom to probe and penetrate, the rhymes and reasons of wise men and women.

"Start with God—the first step in learning is bowing down to God; only fools thumb their noses at such wisdom and learning." (Proverbs 1:2-7 MSG)

Every proverb has a specific topic aimed to benefit the well-being of a specific group of people. The book of Proverbs should be a learning curriculum for every family. After all, the home is the real classroom of life!

Women's issues are scattered throughout the Bible and Proverbs, and all of them should be studied diligently. Proverbs 31 primarily addresses womanhood, and contains "smarts" that are concentrated, conveyed to women specifically. Teachable women will follow its admonition in order to adhere to God's plan for them in life.

The Virtuous Woman Is

SCARCE

WHO CAN FIND A VIRTUOUS WOMAN?

Scarce simply means "limited in small quantity in proportion to the demand; not easily to be procured; rare; uncommon"[1]

While there are about four *billion* women in the world, there is a scarcity of virtuous ones. Even a simple review of commodity theory shows that the scarcer something is, the greater its value. This theory purports that scarcity enhances the value (or desirability) of anything that can be possessed or is useful. To put it another way, any commodity will be valued to the extent that it is unavailable.

Now while we know that women can *never* and *must never* be referred to as a commodity, it's also a fact that *virtuous* women are scarce. Virtuous women are not for sale, cannot be bought, manipulated, maneuvered, coerced, used, or abused. In any situation in which she can make a choice, the virtuous woman refuses to be the pawn of men, the victim of cultural propaganda, or the slave of immoral coercion. They were born free and God, their Creator, intends them to stay free. Their femininity is *not* a disadvantage nor does it indicate inferiority to men. A woman is simply, a "wombed man."

When there is a scarcity of water, every drop counts. In a culture that has become increasing evil, every virtuous woman counts inestimably! Virtuous women not only save lives; they can save a culture. But they are scarce!

"The Scarcity of Flowers in the society made guys settle for weeds and grasses.... Trust me, I'll rather import a Rose than be contented with thorns."[2] — Goals Rider

The Virtuous Woman Is

VALUABLE

...FOR HER WORTH IS FAR ABOVE RUBIES.

Not so long ago somebody brought me a ruby ring and asked me what it was worth. I said I didn't know but that I would take it to a gemologist who was a friend of mine. The stone was about five carats, and he told me that it was worth a lot if it were real.

A genuine ruby of that size would have been worth about *six times the price of a diamond of comparable size*. Proverbs 31 says: A woman's value is not that of one ruby—but many!

As George Chapman declared, "Let no man undervalue the price of a virtuous woman's counsel."[3] They are the ones who are valuable to husbands, children, and society.

William Ross Wallace penned it best in his poem entitled, "The Hand That Rocks the Cradle Is the Hand That Rules the World."[4] In this beautiful poem from the late 1800s, Wallace extolled the importance of a mother's role and the effect she had on every child. I am convinced that the women of the future will determine the future of America and the world. And it is the Bible, the Holy Scriptures, the inerrant Word of God, that places women in the highest place and status that can be found anywhere. It was Mary that did more for womanhood than all others. It was in Mary that God placed Himself. What esteem! What regard! What reverence for women!

Virtuous women are Bible-thinking women. They know how to win at life. They know how to respond to all of life's situations, and teach others to do the same. That is called wisdom—no small factor in Proverbs.

Wisdom and folly are represented by two very different women in the Bible. Lady Wisdom (in contrast to Madam Folly) is so valuable she can only be compared to rubies.

The Virtuous Woman Is

TRUSTWORTHY

THE HEART OF HER HUSBAND SAFELY TRUSTS HER, SO HE WILL HAVE NO LACK OF GAIN.

This is not a misplaced trust. Her husband can really trust her. When you just meet someone, you may think they are really wonderful but you may be wrong. You aren't acquainted with the choices they make. Not so with the husband of a virtuous woman.

Her husband truly knows his wife. Through their close relationship as they live day after day and year after year, he can trust her.

In fact, "he can *safely* trust her," not just trust her, but confidently do so. He doesn't need anything else. The *Amplified* says it this way: "The heart of her husband trusts in her confidently and relies on and believes in her securely, so that he has no lack of [honest] gain or need of [dishonest] spoil."

If a man has a virtuous woman, he possesses a treasure worth far more than many rubies: She is trustworthy. Imagine having no fear of disloyalty or desertion. Instead, she is tried and true, reliable and honest; she is a refuge for her husband.

Adjectives fail but here are a few: She is authentic, sincere, consistent, considerate, available, reliable, dependable, principled, upright, steadfast, tested, tried, and proven. Best of all, she is an honest and effective communicator.

The word *reputation* refers to the way other people regard us. The word *character* refers to what we *really* are deep inside. Billy Graham wisely said this: "When wealth is lost, nothing is lost; when health is lost, something is lost; *when character is lost, all is lost*."[5]

If we were to create a "valuable" characteristics list, trustworthiness would top the list.

The Virtuous Woman Is

FAITHFUL

SHE DOES HIM GOOD AND NOT EVIL ALL THE DAYS OF HER LIFE!

Disloyalty, infidelity, adultery, cheating, deceit, and desertion have become pretty commonplace.

Who can tally the pain of betrayal? Who can you trust? A virtuous woman. She is faithful, loyal, devoted, true-blue, and steadfast in all her affections.

Faithfulness is not a part-time quality. It is said that a broken clock is right twice a day, but I don't know anyone willing to actually wear a broken watch. We want to be able to glance at our watch and get the real time.

Love never fails—never! "Love knows no limit to its endurance, no end to its trust, no fading of its hope.… It is, in fact, the one thing that still stands when all else has fallen" (1 Corinthians 13:7–8a PHP).

In marriage, a man and a woman stand before God and others that gather to witness as they make their vows to God about one another. Those vows are usually something like this: "I will love you and cherish you until death do us part. I forsake all others and will keep myself only unto you, as long as we both shall live."

Vows don't change with circumstances. "For better for worse, for richer or poorer, in sickness or in health" is the vow we made. Psalm 15:4 applauds the one "who keeps his word even when it hurts, and does not change their mind" (paraphrased). In other words, we are to keep our word even if it costs us.

Marriage is a sacred covenant. It's not like one of those contracts in which the large print commits to something that the small print takes away. There is no small print. To the valiant man or the virtuous woman, the "D word" is not in their vocabulary. Divorce is not an option.

The Virtuous Woman Is

INDUSTRIOUS

SHE SEEKS WOOL AND FLAX,
AND WILLINGLY WORKS WITH HER HANDS.

She is a go-getter! When it says she seeks wool and flax, it means she is looking for work. She doesn't work because she must. She does it willingly, intentionally. She seeks it because she is stable, careful, and diligent.

This doesn't just describe her mind. She isn't just entrepreneurial in a business sense; she is also willing to work with her hands. Later in the chapter, it says, "She stretches out her hands to the distaff, and her hand holds the spindle" (Proverbs 31:19).

A *distaff* is a stick that holds unspun fibers so they can be spun onto a spindle. The whole process of weaving cloth took time, skill, and preparation. Before any garment could be sewn, this job had to be completed. A virtuous woman has no problem with tasks like this. She rolls up her sleeves and gets things done.

This is the opposite of slothfulness (named after that famously slow animal that spends most of its life just hanging upside-down). A person called a *sloth* is lazy and reluctant to work.

In contrast, the virtuous woman's heart follows these biblical admonitions: "Whatever your hand finds to do, do it with your might" (Ecclesiastes 9:10) and "Whatever you do, do it heartily, as to the Lord and not to men" (Colossians 3:23).

She always rises above—not simply to please others, but to please God. She takes the initiative and follows through. She knows the dangers of mediocrity and settling for wishful thinking without action, but consciously chooses to accomplish her calling instead.

Her feet are on the ground. She is in motion. Better get out of her way or you might get run over.

The Virtuous Woman Is

RESOURCEFUL

SHE IS LIKE THE MERCHANT SHIPS; SHE BRINGS HER FOOD FROM AFAR.

Resourcefulness has many applications. Many of us like the idea of shopping around, and maybe even think: *Hey, I must be a virtuous woman. I shop.* She is not just a shopper. She is a thrifty shopper. She is watchful over the economy of her household and careful not to spend unnecessarily.

She examines merchandise to make sure it is good before she purchases it, and looks for the best buy. As a meticulous person, she looks for bargains, demonstrating frugality and resourcefulness. She stretches her money and researches ingredients for quality assurance. The "organic" or "natural" designation on a package is not enough. She checks it out.

A virtuous woman is nutritionally conscientious about what she feeds herself and others. She is educated about organic and natural foods.

She also makes good use of what others may not value.

I had a friend in Houston, Texas, who as a boy picked up junk that others threw away because they could not see its value. He fixed what was broken; cleaned what was dirty; painted what was rusty. He salvaged stuff, transformed it into something of value, and sold it. Today he is a multi-millionaire plus some. How? Resourcefulness!

The resourceful woman is full of practical ingenuity too. She sees possibilities, knows how to overcome lack, and turns deficiencies into efficiencies and sufficiencies! She wastes not!

The Virtuous Woman Is

THOUGHTFUL

SHE ALSO RISES WHILE IT IS YET NIGHT, AND PROVIDES FOOD FOR HER HOUSEHOLD, AND A PORTION TO HER MAIDSERVANTS.

The Bible warns about too much sleep: "A little sleep, a little slumber, a little folding of the hands to sleep—so shall your poverty come" (Proverbs 6:10–11a).

The virtuous woman is awake before anybody else—even when it is still dark out, because she is so industrious. She is a woman with a mission. She is a woman with vision and goals. She is going somewhere and gets right on it at the earliest part of her day.

Her motivation to do this is her desire to care for others. The reason she is up before everyone else is to get meals ready for her household, for those for whom she is responsible. Interestingly, the Scripture seems to indicate that when the word *food* is used it's often referring to spiritual food—food for the soul, not just physical food. She wants to provide her husband, her children, and all those around her with moral and encouraging spiritual food. She has gone to great lengths to plant healthy and holy thoughts in the hearts of her children. She maintains an honest and kind relationship with her husband. She is going to have something encouraging to say to everyone. She is always preparing spiritual food for those around her.

Oh, the power of a sound mind fed with noble and inspiring God-based thoughts! A virtuous woman follows Philippians 4:8. Here's a paraphrase:

Whatever is True
Whatever is Honest
Whatever is Just
Whatever is Pure
Whatever is Lovely
Whatever is of Good Report
Whatever is Virtuous
Whatever is Praiseworthy
Think on these things.

The Virtuous Woman Is

SAVVY IN BUSINESS

SHE CONSIDERS A FIELD AND BUYS IT...

An entrepreneur is "one who creates a product on his own account; whoever undertakes on his own account an industrial enterprise in which workmen are employed."[6] They own and run a business. The virtuous woman does not sit around wasting time.

Getting into business is relatively easy. *Staying* in business is a different story. It requires business savvy. *Savvy* means "comprehension; knowledge of affairs; mental grasp."[7]

However, her expertise is in business and economics. She has learned the basics of

- Envisioning
- Planning
- Funding
- Staffing
- Directing
- Maintaining

She looks at a piece of real estate and with her own hand, increases its worth and sells it for a profit. The Bible clearly attests that a godly woman can buy, sell, and prosper in her business dealings.

However, a virtuous woman does not do business at the expense of her home and family. She is a multi-tasker.

In fact, this Proverbs 31 gal may have several businesses going on at one time, including manufacturing. She understands both macro- and micro- economics which translates into wise domestic and business management skills.

She really understands: "If your outgo exceeds your income, your upkeep becomes your downfall." The virtuous woman lives within her means but also knows how to enlarge her means if needed.

The Virtuous Woman Is a

HORTICULTURALIST

...FROM HER PROFITS SHE PLANTS A VINEYARD!

Horticulture is the art of cultivating plants and managing gardens. This includes growing flowers, fruits, vegetables, and herbs.

The virtuous woman is not a fast food buff. She is smart and properly suspicious of processed foods or previously cooked foods that have changed in nutritional composition in the process.

She knows that sugar is the most delicious poison so she knows the dangers of sugary drinks, candies, and savory snacks.

Organic is more than a byword, more than a USDA label. (And she is a label reader—all the time, every time.) She's on the alert for foods grown with synthetic chemicals, pesticides, and genetically modified organisms. Nutrition is fundamental. She knows God is smart and put everything we need, even our medicine, in our food. (See Ezekiel 47:12.)

With a shortage of pesticide-free and additive-free foods, the virtuous woman develops an aptitude for growing her own plants. She's got a green thumb, so named as a description of fingers that often handled earthenware pots which had algae growing on their underside.

Her food is fresher; she controls what goes into and on top of her dishes. Her choices are more cost-effective, and she cares for her garden so she is able to select appropriately to her family's needs. She benefits the whole family and enjoys sharing the work of her hands with many others in her broader sphere of influence. Horticulture could be spelled H-E-A-L-T-H.

The Virtuous Woman Is

ATTRACTIVE
TO HER HUSBAND

SHE GIRDETH HER LOINS WITH STRENGTH! KJV

We live in a culture that seems to be all about sex and sexuality. You don't have to watch more than a few television commercials before you begin to understand the phrase "sex sells." Yet amidst a highly sexualize culture, the virtuous woman can be both attractive and desirable to her husband, be beautiful and live beautifully in the world without compromising her values, her grace, and her style.

God created sex for our pleasure. To maximize that pleasure, He has given us guidelines for how to have a lifetime of intimacy and joy. The virtuous woman knows that she is attractive both inside and out, yet does not feel the need to compare herself to others or to flaunt her beauty in a way that draws attention to her frame.

When Proverbs says, "she girdeth her loins," it is referring to the procreative parts of the body that produces offspring, which is also the part we cover by clothing. What highlights a woman's virtue when it comes to her desire for intimacy and connection is that it is grounded in love and guided by wisdom. It is not displayed or shared freely with outsiders, but it is guarded and practiced within the sacred halls of marriage. The virtuous woman knows the right moral disposition: "Marriage is honorable among all, and the bed undefiled" (Hebrews 13:4a). Marriage is to be esteemed as precious, especially dear, and honored.

The virtuous woman is indeed beautiful inside and out and focuses her desire toward her husband.

(More information on this topic can be found here: NothingButTheTruth.org/VirtuousWoman)

The Virtuous Woman Is

PHYSICALLY STRONG

...AND STRENGTHENS HER ARMS...

She takes the time to keep herself in good physical condition. Her physical strength and nutrition are very important to her. Why? She wants to be at her best!

"For bodily exercise profits a little, but godliness is profitable for all things" (1 Timothy 4:8).

The Message renders it thus: "Workouts in the gymnasium are useful, but a disciplined life in God is far more so, making you fit both today and forever." This woman maintains a healthy balance in her life. She is both spiritually and physically strong.

Some exercise for vain reasons. They want to look good so they are admired. For these motivations, physical beauty can cause more damage than good.

However, exercising for good health has many positive benefits: It increases our metabolism, controls weight, combats diseases, boosts energy, improves one's mood, develops strength and endurance, keeps us limber, increases coordination and balance, improves digestion, decreases stress, helps us sleep, controls blood pressure, lowers cholesterol, improves self-esteem, provides opportunities to listen to something, and can be a platform for meeting new people.

The virtuous woman is a strong woman.

The Virtuous Woman Is

CONSCIENTIOUS

SHE PERCEIVES THAT HER MERCHANDISE IS GOOD: AND HER LAMP DOES NOT GO OUT BY NIGHT. SHE STRETCHES OUR HER HANDS TO THE DISTAFF, AND HER HAND HOLDS THE SPINDLE.

To be conscientious has two meanings: to be "influenced by conscience; governed by a strict regard to the dictates of conscience, or by the known or supposed rules of right and wrong" and "characterized by a regard to conscience"[8] in doing one's work well and thoroughly.

It has been said that "the devil is in the details." However, this woman finds multiple blessings in the details. She deals with each piece, giving attention to the minute particulars of each.

She is exacting, discriminating, and precise, minding all her Ps and Qs.

She is *not* careless, indifferent, unscrupulous, or irresponsible. She does whatever it takes in terms of time and energy to accomplish a task. There is no passive resistance, escape mechanisms, side-stepping, shirking, or laziness here.

The virtuous woman confronts problems, but does so in a careful manner, so as not to be offensive or obnoxious. She does not use what psychologists describe as maladaptive coping in which a person changes their behavior to avoid thinking about, feeling, or doing difficult things. She tackles things head on.

This remarkable virtue can precipitate a lot of criticism, but it is always from those who aren't conscientious themselves. How should a husband respond to his conscientious wife? How about with gratitude? Appreciation? Honor? Respect? Maybe all of the above?

This wife is her husband's helper, filling in for that which he lacks.

By now, you are probably wishing there was a book like this for men! There probably is.

The Virtuous Woman Is

SENSITIVE, GENEROUS, CARING

SHE EXTENDS HER HAND TO THE POOR; YES, SHE REACHES OUT HER HANDS TO THE NEEDY.

Who cares? She does! She really cares. No faking here! She's the real deal.

To care means to give "attention or heed; caution; regard; heedfulness; watchfulness" for another.[9] Her caring is not motivated by personal benefit or profit.

"Some have compassion, making a difference" (Jude 1:22 KJV). Compassion is her true motivation. She will do what it takes to heal the hurts of another. That means that she is sensitive and has a delicate and profound appreciation for the feelings and condition of others. She is gentle, not harsh.

"Finally, all of you be of one mind, having compassion for one another; love as brothers, be tenderhearted, be courteous; not returning evil for evil or reviling for reviling, but on the contrary blessing, knowing that you were called to this, that you may inherit a blessing. For 'He who would love life and see good days, let him refrain his tongue from evil, and his lips from speaking deceit'" (1 Peter 3:8–10).

The virtuous woman knows the difference between the truly poor and the slothful person, and differentiates care from enabling.

Note that this woman "extends" and "reaches out"! Her scope for care includes those beyond her own family.

She recognizes that all she has really belongs to God, so it should be used for His purposes. Therefore she is not grasping, but open-handed and generous.

SHE IS NOT AFRAID OF THE SNOW FOR HER HOUSEHOLD: FOR ALL HER HOUSEHOLD ARE CLOTHED WITH SCARLET.

"Be prepared" is the Boy Scout's motto. It means that we should always be ready to do what is necessary to help others.

Nobody, absolutely nobody, fills those shoes better than the virtuous woman.

"Prepared" means "to fit, adapt, or qualify for a particular purpose or condition; to make ready; to put into a state for use or application"[10] and can be applied mentally, spiritually, and physically. The virtuous woman understands the future actions that may be required and she is up to the task. No surprise there!

God helps her. "The preparations of the heart belong to man (or woman), but the answer of the tongue is from the Lord. Commit your works to the Lord, and your thoughts will be established" (Proverbs 16:1, 3).

She thinks about what she is doing and plans accordingly; and she does so confidently because God is her Helper.

She has insight into what may be coming. This is helpful overall because it is usually easier to prevent something bad from happening than to deal with the fallout afterward.

We learn from the Proverbs 31 woman that we need not fear. How does the virtuous woman escape fear? Through preparation.

"For God has not given us a spirit of fear; but of power and of love and of a sound mind" (2 Timothy 1:7).

"There is no fear in love" (1 John 4:18). This woman is fearless because she lives love and is prepared to do whatever necessary to help others.

The Virtuous Woman Is

MODEST

SHE MAKES TAPESTRY FOR HERSELF...

What a woman is within herself always manifests on the outside. Women who dress like prostitutes are indicating their moral condition. If it isn't for sale, it shouldn't be advertised.

We dress the way we think. We feel the way we dress and we act the way we feel. Think about that for a moment.

If you get out of bed in the morning and leave your pajamas on until noon, you are not likely to get a lot of work done. You will act the way you feel: laid-back, casual, even lazy. But if your feet hit the floor, and you scrub your face, get cleaned up, and prepare for the day, you will dress accordingly. That choice will affect how you feel. Clothing is important. The virtuous woman is a modest dresser. Her body is not for sale. It's not a grafitti board, a playground, or an amusement park.

We already reviewed the devastation that comes from public undressing when we learned about Madam Folly in Proverbs 7. Dressing to seduce is not part of the virtuous woman's life. She's not interested in doing that.

It's a fact that men are more visually aroused than women. It doesn't take much for them to give in to their own immoral imaginations. She who provokes to lust is surely guilty of the crime of which she is the guilty cause. The virtuous woman covers up, and doesn't sell herself cheap. Men will have no occasion or cause for temptation by her appearance. If they have a problem, it will be their own.

The Virtuous Woman Is

WELL-DRESSED

HER CLOTHING IS FINE LINEN AND PURPLE.

She's not just modest, she's elegant. Fine linen is costly and lasts a long time, and purple is a regal color.

There are four purposes for clothing.

First of all, clothing protects us.

Shoes protect our feet, while clothes protect our bodies from the elements or whatever may cause injury.

Clothing is also a symbol.

The policeman's uniform represents his authority. In the hospital, medical health professionals wear particular clothes that denote their many and varied jobs.

Our clothing also differentiates gender.

The Bible says it is an abomination for a man to wear a woman's clothing and vice versa. The virtuous woman enjoys being feminine. She dresses in a way that not only conveys her femininity, but symbolizes what she thinks of herself.

Another purpose is modesty. We cover the parts of ourselves that are private and more delicate.

Because the virtuous woman is confident in her identity as a woman, she does not need to attract others by exposing herself.

The pressure on women today to dress immodestly to be accepted by society is certainly an unrighteous thing. The virtuous woman doesn't showcase her body. Her value is far above rubies and she knows it. She is self-contained, self-established, and self-fulfilled because she has virtue.

She has class and fashion, and never looks cheap or shabby.

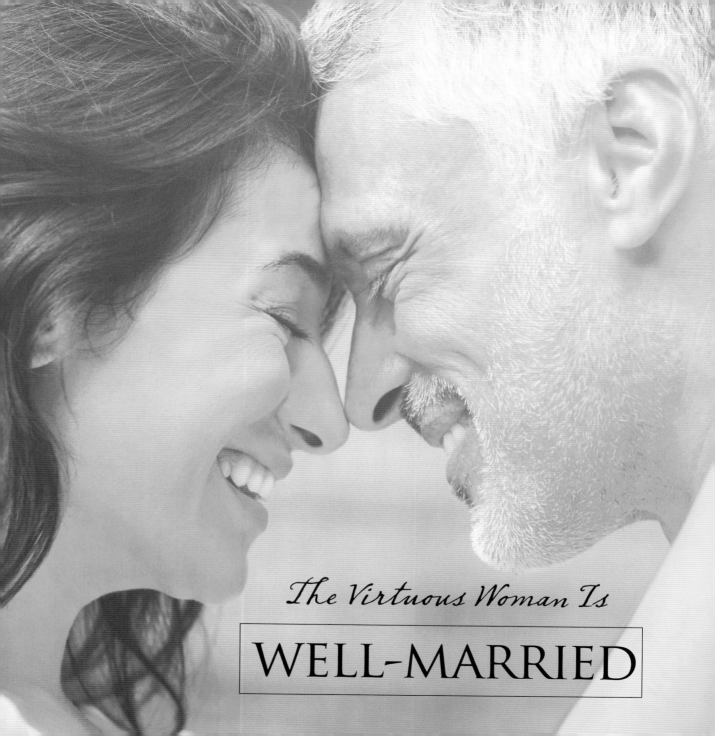

The Virtuous Woman Is

WELL-MARRIED

HER HUSBAND IS KNOWN IN THE GATES,
WHEN HE SITS AMONG THE ELDERS OF THE LAND.

The virtuous woman is smart enough to:

- Never marry a stranger
- Never marry for appearances
- Never marry a deceiver
- Never marry an atheist
- Never marry what she hopes he'll be
- Never trust without verifying

She will never say, "This marriage was a mistake." She believes this: "When you make a vow to God, do not delay to pay it; for He has no pleasure in fools. Pay what you have vowed—better not to vow than to vow and not pay" (Ecclesiastes 5:4-5).

Marriage is a lifetime partnership, a covenant; she made a vow before God to her husband and in front of witnesses.

In ancient times, all cities were walled. The only access to the city was through its gates.

Government officials had offices at the gates so they could control who came in (immigration), what came in (imports), and what left (exports). The gates were political and governmental centers and elders were in charge.

A virtuous woman looks for a man who will have virtuous influence on others. (We could use a big fat dose of this in our country right about now.)

Washington, D.C., is the gate of America. Each state has a capital, a governor, and staff who control the gates. Likewise, our counties, cities, towns, and villages have a similar structure. Each home has "gates" (parental controls) that decide who and what is or is not allowed in: physically or electronically.

The virtuous woman wants a valiant man who will stand guard for what is right.

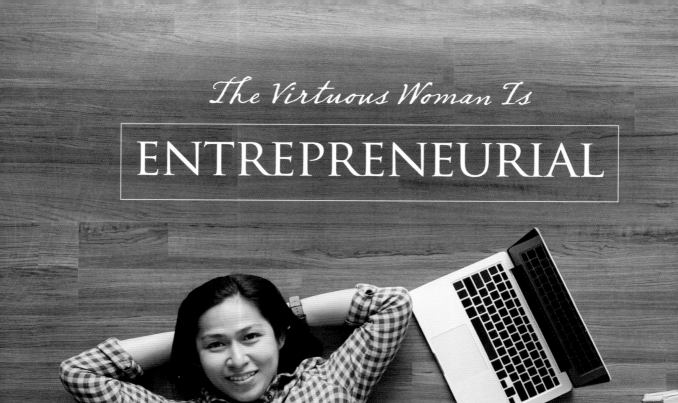

The Virtuous Woman Is

ENTREPRENEURIAL

SHE MAKES LINEN GARMENTS, AND SELLS THEM; AND SUPPLIES SASHES TO THE MERCHANT.

We've already learned that the Proverbs 31 woman not only delved into real estate, but also had oversight of the manufacturing, sales, and delivery processes.

Virtuous women are well-suited to this because as mothers they have learned to multitask. Let's face it. They nurse, cook, teach, play, housekeep, babysit, clean, chauffeur, wash laundry, and keep accounts, not to mention look after their husbands, and much, much more.

Entrepreneurship is the creation of value. An entrepreneur is an innovator, and runs her business with knowledge, professionalism, good communication and social skills, and of course, the ability to learn. Zig Ziglar puts it this way: "If you are not willing to learn, no one can help you. If you are determined to learn, no one can stop you."[11]

When working, we learn that the number one requirement in any enterprise is the ability to get along with others. It takes a team.

This woman is unwilling to let fear destroy her creativity. Like each of us, she is born with a God-given Embedded Natural Ability (ENA) which God deposited in her before she was born.

Upon discovery of her ENA, she applies it to business. Many have never discovered their ENA so they stumble through life without realizing the embedded wealth they have. The giver chooses the gift; and in your case (as in mine), the gifting came from the smartest, most loving Person in the universe, God Himself.

(Details on your ENA can be found in the author's book titled *Why You Were Born*.)

The Virtuous Woman Is

CHARACTER-BASED

STRENGTH AND HONOR ARE HER CLOTHING...

Character describes the moral and mental qualities that are strongly developed or strikingly displayed in a person and have become the essence of that person's established *modus operandi*.

Each of us has a basic structural motivation, a foundational disposition that determines our thinking and responses to each and every life situation.

For example, if a person has anger issues, their thinking will always be contaminated by their anger. Decisions will be distorted because their anger will manipulate, and even bypass, their logic. This is true of envy, jealousy, malice, and so on.

In contrast, the virtuous woman has developed a core of character qualities which empower her moral compass.

Consequently, her every response is controlled and proper, free of selfish motivations, providing the highest possible outcome for all in every situation, whether friendly or hostile.

Character is:

- Birthed in the heart
- Learned from the instruction of wisdom and the example of Jesus
- Stored in the mind
- Maintained by discipline
- The prime controller of all behaviors
- The responder rather than the reactor to all life situations
- Proven to be superlative in real life

Character determines outcomes in the present and in the future.

"Strength and dignity are her clothing and her position is strong and secure; she rejoices over the future" (Verse 25 AMP).

The Virtuous Woman Is

FORWARD-THINKING

SHE SHALL REJOICE IN TIME TO COME...

Lazy is not on this woman's agenda. She's proactive, forward-thinking, and a planner. She creates or controls situations by taking the initiative over events, anticipating problems rather than simply reacting to them after they have occurred.

The virtuous woman is an innovator. She makes things happen.

Unfortunately, this makes some people feel insecure, even usurped. Sorry, Mister or Missus Insecurity, you should feel blessed and honored to know her.

The virtuous woman is the true feminist. She will not intrude forcibly or illegally or without just cause. She assumes no unjust rule or authority over others. She does not appropriate wrongfully. It's her creativity that inspires her forward, even to novel achievements. She always stays within her lines of designated authority. She is usually a quick thinker as well as a vigorous performer.

Her attitude for the future is positive and optimistic. She believes the promises of God and believes what William Carey, the famous missionary to India, said: "The future is as bright as the promises of God."[12]

Because of her faith in the promises of God, she

- is a willing and able worker who

- doesn't waste time,

- accepts no excuses, and

- is not easily distracted.

The future of this forward-thinking, well-planned woman is full of joy!

The Virtuous Woman Is

WISE

SHE OPENS HER MOUTH WITH WISDOM…

Wisdom is the ability to see and respond to all life's situations from God's accurate point of view. The Bible personifies wisdom as a woman, not a man. Note this example from Proverbs 4: "Get wisdom! Get understanding! Do not forget, nor turn away from the words of my mouth. Do not forsake *her*, and *she* will preserve you; love *her*, and *she* will keep you. Wisdom is the principal thing; therefore get wisdom. And in all your getting, get understanding. Exalt *her*, and *she* will promote you; *she* will bring you honor, when you embrace *her*" (Proverbs 4:5–8, emphasis mine).

Many a theologian has vainly attempted to explain God's choice, but if you ask any woman, she could probably give you ten good reasons in short order.

There is no doubt that a virtuous woman is intelligent and wise. She's just plain smart.

Perhaps motherhood demands it, and God embedded these capabilities in women for that daunting task. Wisdom is essential for it.

Perhaps it's because virtuous women listen to God more readily than men. When Jesus was hauled up before Pilate, his wife sent a message to Pilate, saying, "Don't get mixed up in judging this noble man" (Matthew 27:19 MSG).

Unfortunately, Pilate listened to the mob instead of his wife. Men should learn to listen to their wives; their wives are given them as helpers (Genesis 2:18).

Men sometimes logically arrive at the wrong conclusions, while women who may not be able to explain something in logical terms, often come to right conclusions. A man who does not listen to his wife is in grave danger, though he may not know it.

The Virtuous Woman Is

KIND

...AND ON HER TONGUE IS THE LAW OF KINDNESS!

To be kind means to "show tenderness or goodness; disposed to do good and confer happiness; sympathetic."[13] This is shown through her friendly, warm-hearted manner towards others with the intent of being helpful and doing them good.

The true feminist is not just kind periodically. For her, kindness is law, a rule of action, a disposition she shows toward everyone in any circumstance, regardless of the way others treat her. She returns kindness for unkindness, failing to allow others to reduce her to their level.

She returns good for evil, even blessings for curses. She chooses to pray for those who are out of order. This is one of her many godlike character qualities. Here's what the Lord Himself taught us:

"But love your enemies, do good, and lend, hoping for nothing in return; and your reward will be great, and you will be sons of the Most High. For He is kind to the unthankful and evil. Therefore be merciful, just as your Father also is merciful" (Luke 6:35–36).

She is kind because she loves greatly, and we are taught in that famous love chapter that "love suffers long, and is kind" (1 Corinthians 13:4).

According to Proverbs 19:22 (TLB), "Kindness makes a man attractive," and this woman is exactly that.

Note that her kindness comes from her tongue, her lips, her words, her speech.

The prophet Isaiah wrote: "The Lord God has given me the tongue of the learned, that I should know how to speak a word in season to him who is weary" (Isaiah 50:4a). The virtuous woman reflects this verse.

The Virtuous Woman Is

FAMILY-CENTERED

SHE WATCHES OVER
THE WAYS OF HER HOUSEHOLD...

God did not design baby factories in which you could dump a little protein into a machine, add hydrogen, oxygen, carbon, nitrogen, and water, crank for two days and pow, out comes a baby.

He designed a father plus a mother plus a loving sexual relationship plus 270 days of waiting and months of feeding, diaper-changing, nourishing, and love. When that part is completed, it's followed by many more loving years of feeding, clothing, training, instructing, discipline, praying, and educating.

No man can do this without a woman, and that woman better be a virtuous one or all is lost for the future. The chain we see of single parenting must be broken by valiant men and virtuous women.

The home is the classroom where life is learned. Either virtues or vice is handed on. To "train up a child in the way he should go" (Proverbs 22:6) requires that you go that way yourself.

The virtuous woman is the model for her children and friends. Without virtue, here's what happens: "Indeed everyone who quotes proverbs will use this proverb against you: 'Like mother, like daughter!' You are your mother's daughter, loathing husband and children" (Ezekiel 16:44–45a).

A boy learns how to treat women by watching how his father treats his mother. Girls learn how to properly respond to their husbands by watching how their mother responds to their father.

All family time must be virtue time! The stakes have never been higher!

The Virtuous Woman Is

MOTIVATED

It's true that direction is more important than speed. But that's no excuse to go slow! Nevertheless, direction must be the top priority. Imagine if a person is motivated to go in the wrong direction. The consequences could be eternal. Off-track can be deadly. Facing the constant barrage of temptations rampant today requires a strong motivation to do the right thing. The virtuous woman has the right stuff.

That's why Priority One for her is "to know wisdom and instruction; to perceive the words of understanding; to receive the instruction of wisdom, justice, judgment, and equity" (Proverbs 1:2–3).

That's how she knows the right way, which enables her to zoom, zoom, zoom! Just as in The Warrior's Creed she can say:

"I am not ashamed! I've stepped over the line. My decision for virtue has been made. I won't look back, let up, slow down, back away, or be still.

"My past is redeemed; my present makes sense; my future is secure. I don't have to be praised, recognized, regarded, or rewarded. My face is set; my gait is fast; my mission is clear; my goal is heaven; my road is narrow; my way is rough; my companions are few but my God is reliable.

"With God's help I will not flinch in the face of sacrifice; hesitate in the presence of the Adversary; negotiate at the table of the Enemy; or ponder at the pool of popularity. I am a disciple of Jesus Christ. I must go until He comes, give until I drop, work until He stops me, and teach until all men know Him and His ways!

"I am on fire!"[14]

The Virtuous Woman Is

PRAISE
WORTHY

HER CHILDREN RISE UP AND CALL HER BLESSED; HER HUSBAND ALSO, AND HE PRAISES HER.

Being praised is never the goal of the virtuous woman. In fact, she would rather defer praise to those who have contributed to her character, virtue, and well-being.

Even so, she will be praised by those who know her well, have spent quality time with her, and benefited by her relationship in ten thousand ways. That means her husband, her children, and those in her sphere will call her blessed.

They bless her because she is a blesser. How did she learn to be such a blesser? From the way God has treated her: "The blessing of the Lord makes one rich, and He adds no sorrow with it" (Proverbs 10:22).

She also learned to be a blesser from the instruction of Jesus. Remember how the crowds gathered on the mountainside when Jesus began His instructions in what I call the Ultimate Life Management System, but which is also known as the Sermon on the Mount? He began with, "Blessed are:

- The poor in spirit…
- Those who mourn…
- The meek…
- Those who hunger and thirst for righteousness…
- The merciful…
- The pure in heart…
- The peacemakers…
- Those who are persecuted for righteousness' sake."

Having learned this, she lives it. Having lived it, everyone is blessed: "Her husband also, and he praises her" (Proverbs 31:28b).

"A virtuous … wife [earnest and strong in character] is a crowning joy to her husband" (Proverbs 12:4 AMP). This is the reason she is praised by her husband. Virtue wins!

MANY DAUGHTERS HAVE DONE WELL,
BUT YOU EXCELL THEM ALL.

Mediocre means ordinary, of middle quality, average, run-of-the-mill, so-so, humdrum, uninspired, and in some contexts, poor quality and second-rate.

Its antonyms describe this woman: excellent, exceptional, extraordinary, first-rate and of course, excelling!

She is all-in! There is nothing lukewarm about her. She is not apathetic, neutral, spiritless, or half-hearted. She follows this dictum regarding her behavior:

> If it is wrong, leave it undone!
> If it be right, do it boldly!

So in what does she excel? It's in the text: "Many daughters have done virtuously, but thou excellest them all" (Proverbs 31:29 KJV). She excels in virtue, conforming to the principles of morality in her life and conduct. What virtues? Aristotle had his seven: trust, compassion, courage, diligence, patience, kindness, and humility.

In contrast to the seven deadly sins are their counterparts: chastity, temperance, charity, diligence, patience, kindness, and humility.

A comprehensive list would require page upon page, but the virtuous woman is focused on all of those.

She is enthusiastic, eager, fervent, passionate, and zealous. Actually the word "enthusiasm" comes from Greek word *theo* meaning God, and *en* meaning "within you." Thus authentic enthusiasm means a rapturously intense feeling that comes from God. Enthusiasm about evil is not only a conundrum, but a contradiction. Make no mistake, this woman has a God-driven enthusiasm about virtue!

The Virtuous Woman Is

GOD-
FEARING

CHARM IS DECEITFUL, AND BEAUTY IS PASSING: BUT A WOMAN WHO FEARS THE LORD, SHE SHALL BE PRAISED.

Vanity is to reach, to clutch, to grasp but to come up empty. What really matters?

Everyone must be a thinker at some time in life. The big questions must be answered: Is it right or wrong? Is this good or evil? Is this from God or Satan? Will I go to heaven or hell? Am I going to live for life now or for life eternal?

There is no room for many mistakes. The stakes are too high for being led astray, deceived, cheated, duped, hoodwinked, or defrauded.

What will we see when we cross the stage of life, stand near the exit, and look back? This woman will *not* see wasted years that grew into decades. Why? Because of the God Factor. She knew Him! She followed Him! She did His bidding! She treated others with the same dignity He treated her. Therefore, *nothing was lost.* Nobody damned! She lived well—with or without man's favor. She acknowledged the vanity of mere outward beauty. She walked in the fear of God!

The fear of God is the continual awareness that we are in the presence of a just and holy God. Every motive within our hearts and every thought we think, as well as every word we speak and every action we take is open before Him and adjudicated by Him. God sees us! We give account to Him and Him alone. She walks as she "ought to walk … to please God, so (she) would abound more and more" (1 Thessalonians 4:1 KJV, addition mine).

Max Lucado wrote that "a woman's life should be so hidden in God that a man has to seek Him in order to find her!"[15]

The Virtuous Woman Is

HONORABLE

GIVE HER OF THE FRUIT OF HER HANDS; AND LET HER OWN WORKS PRAISE HER IN THE GATES.

To be worthy of honor is more important than to be honored. It's great to be honored, but whence cometh honor?

To be worthy of honor is a matter of choosing and living virtuously. To be honored is a choice made by others; the highest form of this is when it comes from God Himself.

"How can you believe, who receive honor from one another, and do not seek the honor that comes from the only God?" (John 5:44).

The most noteworthy attribute of this woman is that she has chosen God's way, all the way. She is honored by God.

Honor from others is based on merit. Here's the proof: "Render therefore to all their due: taxes to whom taxes are due; customs to whom customs; fear to whom fear; honor to whom honor" (Romans 13:7).

The virtuous woman is due the honor she receives. She has earned it; she deserves it, and is not honored briefly but for the duration: "A gracious woman retains honor" (Proverbs 11:16a).

The women of the future will determine the future of this world. It is the Bible that sets women in the highest place and status that they could ever be found, the place of honor!

"So whoever cleanses himself [from what is ignoble and unclean, who separates himself from contact with contaminating and corrupting influences] will [then himself] be a vessel set apart and useful for honorable and noble purposes, consecrated and profitable to the Master, fit and ready for any good work" (2 Timothy 2:21 AMP).

How to Become a

VIRTUOUS WOMAN

The first step to become virtuous is to **become vertically connected and responsible to your Creator!**

Remember, He fathered you. You are here because God wanted you here. It's true that a man and woman got together and produced a baby, but God is the One who put the person, you, inside the baby. People can make babies, but they can't make people. "Know that the Lord, He is God; it is He who has made us, and not we ourselves; we are His people and the sheep of His pasture" (Psalm 100:3).

Jesus taught us to pray like this: "Our Father in heaven, hallowed be Your name" (Matthew 6:9).

Next, zealously **allow Jesus to come into your life as your Lord and Master**. He alone must become your Life Manager. We do as He says. We live according to His instructions and power.

To do that, **ask for and receive forgiveness, cleansing, and recovery** from all past sin, pride, narcissism, and iniquity. "Ask, and it will be given to you … for everyone who asks receives" (Luke 11:9–10). "If we confess our sins, He is faithful and just to forgive us our sins and to cleanse us from all unrighteousness" (1 John 1:9).

Jesus made all this possible for you. That's why we call Him Savior.

Recognize that you have a fresh start and a clean slate. Everything has become new.

"Therefore, if anyone is in Christ, he (she) is a new creation; old things have passed away; behold, all things have become new" (2 Corinthians 5:17, additions mine).

Forgiven + Cleansed = New Life = ReBorn

My help comes
from the Lord,
which made
heaven and
earth.

PSALM

— 121:1 —

Begin to daily ask God for His help. That's called praying. He will give you the power to do right. That is called grace.

Now that your heart is right, **concentrate on your thinking.** Learn to think God's way about every subject in your life and every person. Read the Bible!

Let your new right thoughts on every subject become your meditation day and night, so your emotions align with your new thinking and become the dynamic energy thrusting you forward in the right directions. Emotions were never intended to be a guidance system; they are the energizers to help us go the right way.

Begin to replan your life based on your virtuous condition.

Then **begin influencing others** into the virtuous movement so they become what you are. (This is a natural process.)

ReBorn + ReThink + ReFocused Emotions + RePlan + ReProduce = Discipleship

Get attached to other virtuous women. Be highly selective of your friends for friends have influence. "He who walks with wise men will be wise, but the companion of fools will be destroyed" (Proverbs 13:20).

Regularly review the twenty-eight qualities of a virtuous woman. Let them be the focus of your progressive development.

If you should fail, do not give up. Contact God! Repent! Be restored! Get back on track! And keep going forward.

(More details on discipleship are available at
  www. NothingButTheTruth.org)

Freedom is not the right to do wrong, but the power to do right.

Concentrate on developing the following fifty character qualities in your life and those of your family. Let these be your family curriculum. Perhaps concentrate on one character quality each week. After memorizing, use it as a point of praise and commendation whenever it is exhibited.

(You can get them printed on individual cards at https://iblp.org/discipleship-tools/biblical-character so each family member can have his or her own.)

Last of all, get involved in a God-honoring, Bible-believing, Bible-teaching church in which you can grow from the presentation of biblical principles and their application. Not all churches are created equal. Beware of fake Christianity!

Remember, virtue depends on character.

When money is lost,
Nothing is lost!
When health is lost,
Something is lost!
When character is lost,
Everything is lost!

Reputation is what others think we are.

Character is what we really are.

Character is our foundational core.

Character is the essence of our being.

Character is our structural motivation.

Virtue
is about
character

You have already learned that one's character covers the moral and mental qualities that are entrenched and strikingly displayed in you. They have become the essence of who you are. For example, we can choose to be one or the other of the following:

- Truthful or Deceptive
- Gentle or Harsh
- Compassionate or Indifferent
- Humble or Proud
- Honoring or Disrespectful

Remember, an excellent character is the norm for a Christian. Our close connection with Jesus Christ cleanses the motivations of our hearts, tames our speech, and is central to having successful relationships. Since He is the essence of all that is right and the evidence of all godliness, His effect on us is that our character is molded into His in such a way that we become a loving and gentle extension of His Person here on earth. Our lives are not only personally satisfying, but also fruitful: this is the Christian reality.

Watch your thoughts for they become feelings, which become words, which become actions, which become habits, which become character, which determine your destiny.

On the following pages you will find a summary of character qualities instructed by wisdom and exhibited by Christ. This is the primary pursuit and agenda of the virtuous woman!

This virtuous and very industrious woman needs physical strength and ability to do the work of her life ... the work of love!

ELIZABETH GEORGE

THE CHARACTER QUALITIES OF A VIRTUOUS WOMAN

Wisdom instead of following Natural Inclinations: She sees and responds to life's situations from God's unbiased and accurate point of view.

Discernment versus Judgment: She has the ability to understand why things happen without condemning.

Discretion versus Simplemindedness: She has the ability to avoid words, actions, and attitudes which could cause unnecessary negative reactions.

Love versus Selfishness: She chooses what is best for others without personal profit as a motive.

Reverence versus Disrespect: She esteems the worth and personal value of others regardless of their maturity level.

Diligence versus Slothfulness: She uses all her energies and skills to achieve that which is worthwhile.

Creativity versus Underachievement: She takes on needs or tasks from a new and different perspective.

Enthusiasm versus Apathy: She has an eager enjoyment of that which lies before both herself and others.

Self-Control versus Self-Indulgence: She has the ability to immediately bring her emotions, desires, and behaviors into line with that which is right.

Dependability versus Inconsistency: She is reliable to do what she has agreed to do in spite of unexpected difficulties.

A virtuous woman is not ruled by her passions but rather she rules her passions!

Patience versus Resistance: She accepts unexpected delays, troubles, or suffering with a positive and optimistic outlook.

Alertness versus Unawareness: She is watchful of that which is taking place around her in order to respond wisely.

Generosity versus Stinginess: She has a readiness to give more of what God has given her than what is strictly necessary.

Joyfulness versus Self-Pity: She expresses great pleasure and happiness because of right relationships with God and others.

Flexibility versus Stubbornness: She is adaptable to unexpected changes in her life without resentment toward God or others.

Availability versus Self-Centeredness: She makes her own schedule and priorities secondary to those she is called to serve.

Endurance versus Giving Up: She possesses inward fortitude to withstand stress and challenges in order to achieve what is best.

Security versus Anxiety: She is free from danger or threat because she knows God is with her.

Thoroughness versus Incompleteness: She gives attention to all the details that are necessary for the successful completion of a task or project.

Orderliness versus Disorganization: She arranges her thoughts, schedule, and surroundings in order to achieve maximum efficiency.

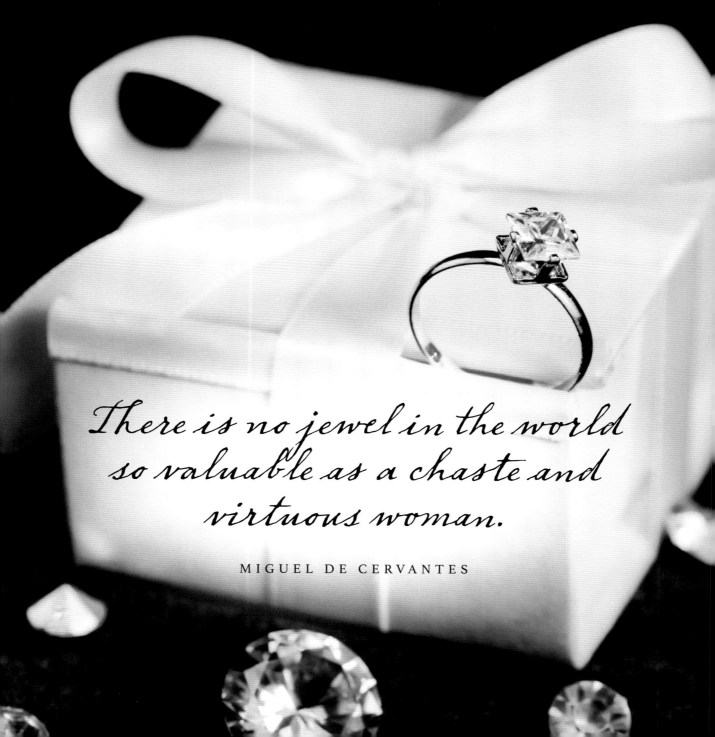

There is no jewel in the world so valuable as a chaste and virtuous woman.

MIGUEL DE CERVANTES

Initiative versus Reactive: She proactively does what needs to be done before necessity dictates an action.

Responsibility versus Unreliability: She knows and does what both God and others are rightfully expecting from her.

Humility versus Pride: She voluntarily takes a lowly position as opposed to being self-exalting.

Decisiveness versus Wavering: She finalizes her decisions based on knowing what is right in any given situation.

Determination versus Weak-mindedness: She exercises resolve to achieve godly goals regardless of opposition.

Justice versus Partiality: She personally weighs evidence to assure that which is pure, upright, and true.

Loyalty versus Unfaithfulness: She uses difficult times or situations as an opportunity to verify her dedication to God, her spouse, her children, and others.

Sensitivity versus Indifference: She picks up on the emotions of others in order not to offend, hurt, or disregard.

Compassion versus Heartlessness: She shows genuine sympathy for others that is demonstrated in meeting their authentic needs.

Gentleness versus Harshness: She shows tenderness and genuine care for the feelings of others that result in meeting their needs.

Deference versus Rudeness: She demonstrates humble respect for others in order not to offend.

Let no man value at a little price a virtuous woman's counsel; her winged spirit is feathered often times with heavenly words ... and, like her beauty, ravishing and pure.

GEORGE CHAPMAN

Meekness versus Anger: She demonstrates long-suffering towards the perceived weaknesses of others.

Obedience versus Deception: She is joyfully compliant to orders or requests of rightful authorities.

Sincerity versus Hypocrisy: She is free to be transparent because she is free from pretense or deceit.

Virtue versus Impurity: She maintains the high moral standards expected by God and defined according to His Word.

Forgiveness versus Bitterness: She deliberately releases others from the harm they have caused her, intentional or not.

Boldness versus Fearfulness: She has confidence and courage without brashness knowing that her opinion is true, right, and just.

Thriftiness versus Extravagence: She shows frugality by not spending for that which is unnecessary, knowing that she will be accountable for the proper use of her time, talent, and treasure.

Contentment versus Covetousness: She realizes that God has already provided everything she needs for her present happiness.

Punctuality versus Tardiness: She shows her dependability, consistency, and her high value of others by being on time.

Caution versus Rash Behavior: She creates a pro/con list before making any decisions in order to identify any problems that could come up.

There is no more beautiful sight than a young woman who glows with the light of the Spirit who is confident and courageous because she is virtuous.

ELAIN S. DALTON

Gratitude versus a Lack of Thanksgiving: She warmly and genuinely expresses to God and others the many ways in which they have or are benefiting her life.

Tolerance versus Prejudice: She joyfully endures the opinions and behaviors of persons or situations with whom or with which she does not agree.

Resourcefulness versus Wastefulness: She is wise and knows clever ways of using her skills and assets which others may have overlooked in order to achieve worthwhile goals.

Persuasiveness versus Ineffectiveness: She convinces others by being able to guide their thinking around mental roadblocks.

Truthfulness versus Deception: She understands and represents facts according to reality and their authentic, unchanging timelessness.

Attentiveness versus Unconcern: She focuses on the words and emotions of others in order to show their worth and respond in applicable and meaningful ways.

Hospitality versus Indifference: She is friendly, congenial, and generous in her reception, provision, and entertainment as well as in the spiritual and social refreshment of her guests, visitors, or strangers.

Merciful versus Exacting: She cares about the well-being of others by relieving their personal pain caused by poverty of body, soul, or finances.

Faith versus Presumption: She visualizes what is right to do in a given situation and actively participates in it.

THE HAND THAT ROCKS THE CRADLE
IS THE HAND THAT RULES THE WORLD

When Napoleon Bonaparte was asked what he considered to be the great need of France, he replied, "Let France have good mothers, and she will have good sons."[16] In an earlier section, I quoted the following poem. Here it is in its entirety.

Blessings on the hand of women!
Angels guard its strength and grace.
In the palace, cottage, hovel,
Oh, no matter where the place;
Would that never storms assailed it,
Rainbows ever gently curled,
For the hand that rocks the cradle
Is the hand that rules the world.

Infancy's the tender fountain,
Power may with beauty flow,
Mothers first to guide the streamlets,
From them souls unresting grow—
Grow on for the good or evil,
Sunshine streamed or evil hurled,
For the hand that rocks the cradle
Is the hand that rules the world.

Woman, how divine your mission,
Here upon our natal sod;
Keep—oh, keep the young heart open
Always to the breath of God!
All true trophies of the ages
Are from mother-love impearled,
For the hand that rocks the cradle
Is the hand that rules the world.

Blessings on the hand of women!
Fathers, sons, and daughters cry,
And the sacred song is mingled
With the worship in the sky—
Mingles where no tempest darkens,
Rainbows evermore are hurled;
For the hand that rocks the cradle
Is the hand that rules the world.[17]

THE MORAL DEGRADATION OF WOMEN IS NOT NEW, AND IT IS THE ULTIMATE FORM OF OPPRESSION.

Randy Alcorn wrote this: "The twentieth century is not the first to see society riddled with immorality. The ancient Greeks elevated loose women, homosexual relations, and pedophilia. The Romans gradually surrendered the strong families and morals that once made them great, replacing them with laxity and weakness. The often-made comparisons between the final years of Rome and modern day America are striking—self-indulgence, political corruption, adultery, homosexuality, sexual orgies, live sex acts in the theater, brutal sports in the arena, and a creeping family deterioration and moral laziness that led to self-destruction."[18]

British historian Arnold J. Toynbee wrote: "Of the twenty-two civilizations that have appeared in history, nineteen of them collapsed when they reached the moral state the United States is in now!"[19]

The loss of core values in America are paralleled to those of the fallen civilizations of Babylon, Persia, Greece, and Rome. George Santayana wrote that "those who cannot remember the past are condemned to repeat it."[20] It seems that we are.

We must all get out of the gutters, men and women alike! May all of us (both genders) strive to be what we should be. Peter Marshall said, "We need women, and men, too, who would rather be morally right than socially correct."[21]

However, this is not just about our culture as a whole; it is about you and yours personally. You may be thinking, Me? I am only one among so very many. What can I do? The answer to those questions follows as does the moment of decision when you, like all women, must decide for yourself.

How important are you? How much influence do you think you can have? What will be the direction of your influence? Towards virtue or vice? You get to decide.

The truth of the matter is that you will influence others for eternity! That's right—not only in this life but forever!

And what about your soul? Did you know that you were born to live forever?

Never minimize yourself and certainly don't let others diminish you. You are someone for whom Christ died! You are notable.

Edward Everett Hale wrote:
> "I am only one, but I am one.
> I cannot do everything,
> But I can do something.
> And what I can do, I ought to do.
> And what I ought to do,
> By the grace of God, I shall do."[22]

Go for it! You are a woman of worth! Keep yourself pure! Live love! Love is the purpose of life. I'd like to leave you with this last passage which is my fervent hope for you!

"How I long that you may be encouraged, and find out more and more how strong are the bonds of Christian love. How I long for you to grow more certain in your knowledge and more sure in your grasp of God Himself. May your spiritual experience become richer as you see more and more fully God's great secret, Christ Himself! For it is in Him, and in Him alone, that men will find all the treasures of wisdom and knowledge. I write this to prevent you from being led astray by someone or other's attractive arguments!" (Colossians 2:1-4 PHP).

Endnotes

1 "Scarce Definition & Meaning." Webster's Unabridged Dictionary. Public Domain. Accessed August 1, 2022. https://www.gutenberg.org/ebooks/29765.

2 GoalsRider. "Quote by GoalsRider." Quoteslyfe. Accessed August 1, 2022. https://www.quoteslyfe.com/quote/The-Scarcity-of-Flowers-in-the-society-246844.

3 Chapman, George. "George Chapman Quotes." BrainyQuote. Xplore. Accessed August 1, 2022. https://www.brainyquote.com/quotes/george_chapman_166068.

4 Wallace, William Ross. "The Hand That Rocks the Cradle." The hand that rocks the cradle - wallace. Accessed August 1, 2022. http://www.potw.org/archive/potw391.html.

5 Graham, Billy. "Billy Graham Quotes." BrainyQuote. Xplore. Accessed August 1, 2022. https://www.brainyquote.com/quotes/billy_graham_161989.

6 "Entrepreneur Definition & Meaning." Webster's Unabridged Dictionary. Public Domain. Accessed August 1, 2022. https://www.gutenberg.org/ebooks/29765.

7 "Savvy Definition & Meaning." Webster's Unabridged Dictionary. Public Domain. Accessed August 1, 2022. https://www.gutenberg.org/ebooks/29765.

8 "Conscientious Definition & Meaning." Webster's Unabridged Dictionary. Public Domain. Accessed August 1, 2022. https://www.gutenberg.org/ebooks/29765.

9 "Care Definition & Meaning." Webster's Unabridged Dictionary. Public Domain. Accessed August 1, 2022. https://www.gutenberg.org/ebooks/29765.

10 "Prepare Definition & Meaning." Webster's Unabridged Dictionary. Public Domain. Accessed August 1, 2022. https://www.gutenberg.org/ebooks/29765.

11 "Zig Ziglar Quotes (Author of See You at the Top) (Page 2 of 15)." Goodreads. Goodreads. Accessed August 10, 2022. https://www.goodreads.com/author/quotes/50316.Zig_Ziglar?page=2.

12 Carey, William. "William Carey Quotes." BrainyQuote. Xplore. Accessed August 10, 2022. https://www.brainyquote.com/quotes/william_carey_191985.

13 "Kind Definition & Meaning." Webster's Unabridged Dictionary. Public Domain. Accessed August 1, 2022. https://www.gutenberg.org/ebooks/29765.

14 Willis, Avery T. "A Quote by Avery T. Willis Jr.." Goodreads. Goodreads. Accessed August 10, 2022. https://www.goodreads.com/

quotes/329151-i-m-part-of-the-fellowship-of-the-unashamed-i-have#:~:text=I%20have%20stepped%20over%20the,back%20away%2C%20or%20be%20still.

15 Lucado, Max. "A Quote by Max Lucado." Goodreads. Goodreads. Accessed August 10, 2022. https://www.goodreads.com/quotes/15202-a-woman-s-heart-should-be-so-hidden-in-god-that.

16 Bonaparte, Napoleon. "A Quote by Napoléon Bonaparte." Goodreads. Goodreads. Accessed August 9, 2022. https://www.goodreads.com/quotes/281899-let-france-have-good-mothers-and-she-will-have-good.

17 Wallace, William Ross. "The Hand That Rocks the Cradle." The hand that rocks the cradle - wallace. Accessed August 1, 2022. http://www.potw.org/archive/potw391.html.

18 Alcorn, Randy. "Immorality & Cultural Decline - Resources." Eternal Perspective Ministries, September 5, 2018. https://www.epm.org/resources/1993/Feb/1/immorality-cultural-decline/.

19 Toynbee, Arnold J. "Of the Twenty-Two Civilizations That Have Appeared in History, Nineteen of Them Collapsed When They Reached the Moral State the United States Is in Now." FixQuotes.com. Accessed August 9, 2022. https://fixquotes.com/quotes/of-the-twenty-two-civilizations-that-have_4361.htm.

20 Walters, Daniel. "Condon Misattributes Quote to Churchill in the State of the City Speech." Inlander. Inlander, August 2, 2022. https://www.inlander.com/Bloglander/archives/2016/02/16/condon-misattributes-quote-to-churchill-in-the-state-of-the-city-speech.

21 Marshall, Peter. "Peter Marshall Quotes (Author of Mr. Jones, Meet the Master)." Goodreads. Goodreads. Accessed August 9, 2022. https://www.goodreads.com/author/quotes/33254.Peter_Marshall#:~:text=It%20needs%20some%20who%20will,morally%20right%20than%20socially%20correct.%E2%80%9D

22 Hale, Edward Everett. "'I Am Only One, but Still I Am One. I Cannot Do Everything, but Still I Can Do Something; and Because I Cannot Do Everything, I Will Not Refuse to Do Something That I Can Do." -Edward Everett Hale." The Foundation for a Better Life. Accessed August 9, 2022. https://www.passiton.com/inspirational-quotes/3660-i-am-only-one-but-still-i-am-one-i-cannot-do.

David L. Johnston lives in Florida with his wife, Judith, whom he adores. His one driving passion is to explain truth in its simplest form to all people. Without the truth, intelligent decisions cannot be made in any area of life.

David has authored numerous titles and concentrated on developing Biblical Life Management Systems. You can follow David at www.NothingButTheTruth.org.

THIS BOOK IS DEDICATED TO THE
VIRTUOUS WOMEN IN MY LIFE:

My Mother Janette McBlain Brown Johnston

My Wife Judith Anne Johnston

My Daughter Faith-Anne Reid

My Daughter Charity Anne Kwapisz

and You, Dear Reader

FOR ADDITIONAL RESOURCES AND HELPS,

PLEASE VISIT OUR WEBSITE:

www.NothingButTheTruth.org/VirtuousWoman